THE BASKET WEAVERS
ARTISANS OF THE SOUTHWEST

Introduction 3

Wicker, Plaiting, and Coil 5
by Laura Graves Allen

Cultural Fiber:
Function and Symbolism in Hopi Basketry 8
by Robert Breunig

One Hundred Years of Havasupai Basketry 14
by Joyce Herold

Western Apache Baskets 23
by Clara Lee Tanner

Museum of Northern Arizona

Photograph courtesy of Jerry Jacka

INTRODUCTION

Basketry has enjoyed a long and constant popularity among prehistoric and contemporary native populations of the Southwest. For the last seven thousand years, the use of baskets has transcended many levels of culture—from strictly utilitarian to social and ceremonial situations. Using techniques unchanged over the millennia, the native peoples of the Southwest have maintained an art form that reflects both an enduring culture and the pressures of social change.

By the early years of this century, many Indians in the Southwest had stopped producing baskets, relying instead on Anglo-made substitutes or on trade with other Native American basketmakers. In other instances, basketry continued as a craft—but in a substantially altered or reduced form.

Since the turn of the century, the sale of baskets to outsiders—tourists and other non-Indians—has had a major impact on the craft. Items produced for decoration rather than utility grew more common, and design and color became ever more important considerations. Native groups that continued to make baskets modified their repertoire in response to these outside influences.

Some groups began producing baskets entirely for commercial outlets by modifying old forms and designs and inventing new ones—such as the Papago lidded baskets with handles, baskets made to look like people and animals, and miniatures of every conceivable form. Other groups, like the Hopi, produced substantially the same type of basket and design as before—merely adding foreign bits and pieces to improve sales. In some instances, the resulting effect has not been totally negative.

As native populations rely more and more on Anglo-produced goods, the decline in craft productions seems to be the inevitable end with only a few holdouts producing baskets either for commission sale or to fulfill the role of artist in their culture. One hopeful sign for the future of basketry as a craft is the current national interest in southwestern art and architecture. However, it seems safe to assume that the basket weaver making baskets for home use will soon be a personality found only in the ethnographic past.

WICKER PLAITING AND COIL

by Laura Graves Allen

The Southwest is one of those places in the world where prehistory does not seem lost in the past. It is possible to sit in a woman's front room and watch her create a wicker plaque—viewing a technology that has not altered significantly for hundreds of years. The tools she uses are simple and have not undergone any appreciable change in form. Bone awls and stone knives have been replaced with metal implements, but teeth and fingernails are still used. Even the plant materials (yucca, rabbitbrush, sumac, and willow) used today are found preserved in many archaeological sites.

The oldest examples of southwestern basketry in existence show the three distinct methods of construction that still characterize the craft today. They are wicker (including twining), plaiting, and coiling. All baskets, whether ancient or modern, are made up of two distinct groups of elements: the warp and weft. The warp functions as the foundation around which the weft material is manipulated. The warp is generally stiffer and more stationary while the weft is more mobile. The warp and weft can be comprised of either single or multiple units; together, they produce both simple and complex patterns.

Wicker

In wicker, the warp and weft are very distinct. The warp, whether single or multiple, is stationary and resembles spokes in a wheel or the ribs of an umbrella. The weft, however, is pliable, can be single or multiple, and is manipulated as a single element.

Hopi weavers lay the starting warps at right angles to each other—and as the weft is laid in, the warps fan out. The number of warps covered by the weft decreases as the basket increases in size until the weave is OVER ONE UNDER ONE. If a larger basket is desired, additional warps can be inserted. In nonutilitarian Hopi wicker, the starting warps are wrapped with the weft material—while the warps are left exposed in utilitarian pieces. When the desired size is attained, the weaver begins the rim by using the exposed warps. Some of the warps are cut off at the rim, and the remaining warps are bent at right angles to parallel the edges of the basket. The rim is then finished with a wrapping of yucca, either dyed in nonutilitarian pieces or undyed (natural) in utilitarian pieces.

Prehistoric and early Hopi weavers rarely, if ever, used color on their wicker baskets. Contemporary nonutilitarian Hopi wicker does not follow this lead. Weavers use natural and aniline dyes to fashion bold geometrics, lifeforms, and kachinas as well as other design elements.

Another form of wicker work found on the Colorado Plateau is twining. Twining is the earliest known basketry technique. It has been recovered from Desert Culture sites that date to 7000 B.C. and has enjoyed a distinct popularity among Native American basketmakers since that time.

As in the wicker technique, the warp, either single or multiple, is stationary. The weft, however, must be multiple since each weft pair twines around each warp element. This technique produces a very strong basket, which may be the reason for its frequent use in the production of utilitarian objects such as pitched water bottles and burden baskets.

Plaiting

In plaiting all elements cross at right angles to each other. There are no distinct warps and wefts in this technique since both sets are manipulated equally. They are the same size and are usually made of the same material. The beginning elements cross at right angles—producing a central cross or other geometric design. The weaving proceeds with the addition of new elements. As the weaving is finished, the basket looks like a flat mat, and it is not until the mat is attached to a frame that it takes on its final shape. The frame is attached by bending the elements over the rim and securing the warps and wefts in place with a twined stitch. Today, plaiting on the Colorado Plateau is limited to the Hopi, who produce plaited yucca baskets on wooden or metal rings.

Patterns are created by varying the weave from plain plaiting (OVER ONE UNDER ONE) to twill plaiting (OVER TWO UNDER TWO, OVER THREE UNDER ONE, etc.). A multitude of geometric designs result from twill plaiting, among them: diagonals, zigzags, and chevrons—in simple and complex treatment. The same geometric designs are amplified today by the use of various natural colors of yucca as well as vegetal and aniline dyes.

WICKER: *The warps radiate from the center like the spokes of a wheel.*

TWINING: *The weft pairs twine around the stationary warps.*

Coil

The most common manufacturing technique encountered on the Colorado Plateau is the method known as coiling. Coiling is actually a sewing technique, but the standard warp and weft terminology applies. The foundation, considered the warp, is encircled as the sewing element, or weft, wraps around and pierces the completed coil beneath. This technique proceeds until the desired size is attained—and the basket is finished. Rim finishes vary from group to group. In contemporary Hopi coiling, the final coil simply tapers off. In some older examples, the bundle is chopped off abruptly and the end left exposed. Navajo coiled baskets exhibit a false braid or herringbone stitch.

Of the three techniques, coiling can be the most expressive in design. Because it is a sewing technique differently colored threads can be changed at will—and designs can be as colorful and elaborate as the craftsman's imagination permits. Geometrics (such as lines, squares, and triangles) form the basis for a variety of motifs. Lifeforms, men and deer, have been very popular among the Western Apache for many decades. Over the years, the Hopi have been quite fond of representing various kachina forms in coil, and one of the most popular today is *Angwusnasomtaqa*, or Crow Mother, with her radial design.

Conclusion

In most cases, environmental constraints influence the manufacturing techniques and materials used in southwestern basketry. In prehistoric times, wicker was virtually unknown in the southern areas of the Southwest—where supple shoots of sumac and rabbitbrush are rare. However, on the Colorado Plateau, coil foundations were made of grass bundles rather than the woody rods found in other locations. Yucca and similar plant materials could be found growing in many areas of the Southwest, and plaiting as a technique is encountered in prehistoric contexts on a pan-Southwest basis. Interestingly enough, these patterns and constraints carried over into the early years of this century. Through a careful analysis of prehistoric and contemporary baskets observers can identify many culturally determined traits. In coiling, for example, the direction in which coiling proceeds (clockwise or counterclockwise) is bound by cultural convention. Whether stitches interlock or not or whether stitches are split or not may appear random—but after careful analysis, most experts believe that these traits are culturally controlled.

Because the Southwest is one of those rare areas where the past and present merge, it is an excellent place to test hypotheses regarding basketry manufacture with the archaeological record and ongoing ethnographic research. New methods of looking at manufacturing techniques are moving from a purely descriptive level to more broadly based cultural analysis.

LAURA GRAVES ALLEN is Anthropology Collections Registrar for the Museum of Northern Arizona.

PLAITING: *The warp and weft cross at right angles and are indistinguishable.*

COILING: *The weft encircles the warp and pierces the coil beneath.*

Cultural Fiber

Function and Symbolism in Hopi Basketry

by Robert Breunig

Crushing kernels of corn into fine meal, a kneeling Hopi woman forces the long flat stone in her hand against a grinding stone with an up-and-down motion of her whole body. When the meal becomes fine, she picks up a brush made of native grasses and sweeps the meal into a pile at the foot of the bin. She then piles the meal on a flat wicker tray.

Before the days of convenient grocery stores, this was the most common daily use of the Hopi wicker plaque. Like most Hopi wicker pieces, the plaque the young woman uses to hold her corn meal is not only striking in its use of color and design but also has a specific name that implies its use. The plaque is called *nguman'inpi,* from *ngumni* (the Hopi word for ground corn meal) and *inpi* (meaning device upon which something is placed).

Hopi women have woven a variety of wicker, plaited, and coiled baskets for centuries with skill and artistry. Some time ago, perhaps in the last century—and for reasons yet unknown, a specialization in basketmaking developed between several of the Hopi mesas. Coiled plaques and baskets became the domain of Second Mesa basket weavers and wicker basketry the province of Third Mesa weavers. Plaited yucca "sifter" baskets continued to be made on a pan-Hopi basis.

Most colorful are the dyed wicker baskets that are woven today in the villages of Hotevilla (Hotvela), Old Oraibi (Orayvi), Kyakqötsmovi (Kiqötsmovi), Bacabi (Paaqavi), and the village of Moencopi (Munqapi) to the west of Third Mesa. This wicker basketry comes in several shapes. Perhaps the most common and best known is

Courtesy Field Museum of Natural History

the *yungyapu* (flat wicker plaque). Similar in form to the *yungyapu* but slightly curved up on its sides is the *yungyapngölökpu* (literally, "wicker plaque which is bent" or shallow wicker plaque). Of apparently recent origin are the *yungyapsivu* (deep wicker basket) and the *yungyapsiphoya* (small wicker basket).

Wicker plaques and baskets have a sunburst warp or foundation with radiating rods of *suuvi* (squaw brush) or *siwi* (dune broom). The weft is made of stripped and dyed branches of *sivaapi* (rabbitbrush). The rabbitbrush weft (today either commercial or vegetal dyes are used) forms the designs on the wicker basketry. Some of these designs are traditional manifestations of nearly subconscious cultural concepts; others are innovations of the artist's imagination. Still others combine several traditional designs or individual and traditional design styles.

There are two ways of naming and therefore describing a wicker plaque or basket. One way specifies the use of the basket; the other refers to its design.

By studying these names, we learn more about how wicker work was actually used and about the rich symbolism of Hopi craftwork.

Some Use Names

Because the use names of Hopi baskets are derived from the context in which they are used, they can be applied to *any* type of basket used in a specific situation and are not restricted to wicker work. In most cases, use names are formed by adding the name of the object that is carried on the plaque or basket with the suffix *inpi*, which means "device upon which something is placed."

The major utilitarian use of the wicker plaque as a tray for holding ground corn has been noted. The plaque was also used to stack or carry piki bread, fruit, or corn still on the cob. In the latter context, the plaque was designated *qa'öinpi*—a device for holding corn.

Plaques also have a variety of ceremonial usages. During several of the major ceremonies, such as the winter solstice (Soyalangw Ceremony) or midsummer Snake Dance, prayer sticks (paaho) are made and then set into a shallow plaque. In this context the plaque becomes a *paho'inpi.* Similarly, before a kachina (katsina) performance, prayer feathers (nakwakwosi) are made and placed on plaques—each of which then becomes a *nakwakwos'inpi.* If a plaque is used during the midwinter Bean Ceremony (Powamuya) to hold special bean sprouts (haru) grown in the ceremonial kiva, it is called *haru'inpi.*

Plaques have a special place in the O'waqölt and Lalkont ceremonies performed by various women's societies. Women dance in a semicircle holding plaques as they sing. As they dance, they hold the plaques in front of them with both hands and gently sway back and forth. These plaques are thus designated *masanpi*—"something with which motion is made." These plaques are then given away at the end of the dances.

Plaques are also given away by the kachinas (katsinam) at the Bean Dance and at the spring and summer kachina dances. At a girl's first Bean Dance, she receives a small flat kachina doll representing Hahayi'wuuti and a yungyaphoya (small wicker plaque). Small plaques are also given to eagles as presents during the summer going-home (Niman) ceremony.

One of the primary ceremonial uses of wicker plaques is during the complex Hopi wedding ceremony. Before the wedding, female neighbors and relatives of the bride gather to make plaques to give to the groom's family. The plaque-making party is called a *yungyap'ayayta.* There is a point during the wedding (which lasts many days) when the bride and her relatives go in a procession to the groom's house. Each one in the procession carries a plaque called a *kongyahompi* or "husband's repayment plaque" in repayment for the bride's wedding robes woven by the groom and his relatives.

Wicker plaques also are used in the performances of the Palhikwmana kachina during winter-night kiva dances at Third Mesa. The Palhikwmanas symbolically grind corn on ancient metates during the course of the dance. At the end of the performance, wicker trays of ground sweet corn, *tosi,* are passed to the visitors—who each take a pinch of corn meal and eat it. In this context, the plaque would be called *tos'inpi.*

Design Names

One of the most common plaque designs is what is known in English as the wedding plaque. This refers to its use at Third Mesa as the principal design for the *kongyahompi* or groom's repayment plaque.

These design terms were collected from three basket weavers at Third Mesa in the fall of 1981.

The design term for this plaque is *nangu' yungyapu,* which means "holding together" or marriage plaque. The name refers to the small rectangles that ring the center of the design and are "held" or linked by a line running between them. This is said by Hopi informants to symbolize the "holding together" of the couple in marriage. An additional term for this plaque is *hahawpi,* which means "device for descending upon." The Hopi say that when a man dies he will ride on his wedding plaque—as on a magic carpet—to the Hopi afterworld beneath the Grand Canyon. (Hopi men jokingly say of this plaque, "Oh, that's my flying saucer, Ha!)"

Tuii'yungyapu in Hopi is "embroidered robe wicker plaque" in English. The *tuui'hi* is the embroidered wedding robe worn on various ceremonial occasions. The plaque design represents the embroidered elements that run along the base of the robe.

Söngö'inyungyapu, or corn cob wicker plaque, has white radiating lines representing corn cobs. One Hopi informant said that the colored bands in between the corn cobs represented the various colors of Hopi corn. Another said they represented a *tatsimrikho,* the banded shinny stick used in a traditional ball and stick game.

Piakyungyapu (caterpillar wicker plaque), *talwiipik'yungyapu* (lightning wicker plaque), and *tota'tsiyungyapu* (slave driver wicker plaque) are all names applied to this plaque. The last term is especially interesting since "tota'tsi" is the name applied to the Spanish Catholic priests who occupied Third Mesa from 1630 until the Pueblo Revolt in 1680.

The tota'tsis coerced the Hopi into building a mission at Old Oraibi, forcing the men to haul mammoth ponderosa and douglas fir logs nearly one hundred miles from the San Francisco Peaks. These logs were used as support beams for the roof of the nave. The mission and its associated complex or *tota'tsikii'at* (slave driver's house) was mazelike in its complexity, and the stepped designs of the plaque echo that structure. (The stepped design can also be seen as a caterpillar or as lightning, which explains the other two names associated with the plaque.)

Muri'ootsokyungyapu literally means "filled-in oblong design wicker plaque." *Muringpu* is the Hopi word for "oblong." At the turn of the century, the Reverend H. R. Voth described this design as *mori* yungyapu or "bean wicker plaque," but it is clear that he misunderstood the name and assumed that the oblong part of the design represented a "mori" or bean. It does not.

Pösalyungyapu means blanket wicker plaque. The pösaala is the striped wool blanket used by Hopi males. Some basketmakers have adapted the colors and designs from these blankets into their basket designs. The stripe of the blanket is reflected in a continuous band around the plaque.

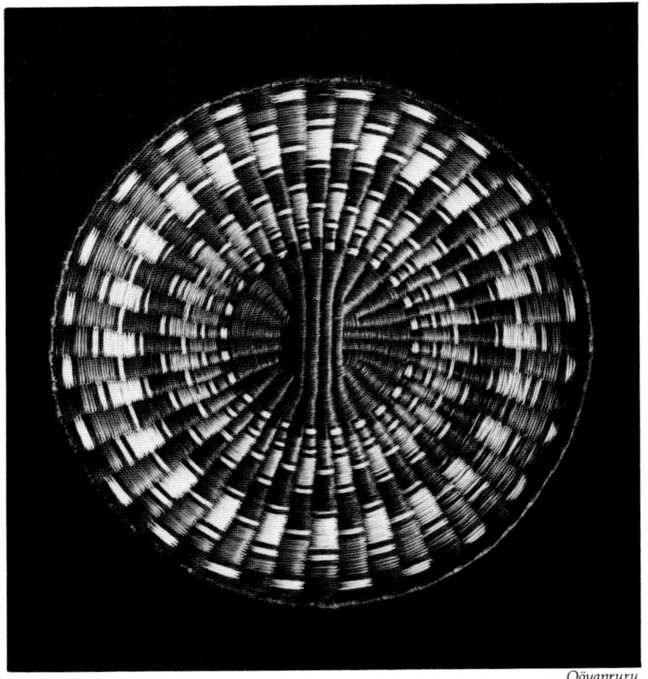

Qöyapruru

Qöyapruru (white showing through) and qöqönyungyapu (circles going round and round plaque) are two distinct designs that are combined in this plaque. The "white showing through" refers to the short white elements that are interspersed throughout the design. They are said to refer to the whites of averted eyes or the whites of just opened eyes. *Qöqön,* or "the circles going round," refers to the concentric bands of color radiating out from the center of the plaque.

Ööqa'yungyapu *Hötapiyungyapu*

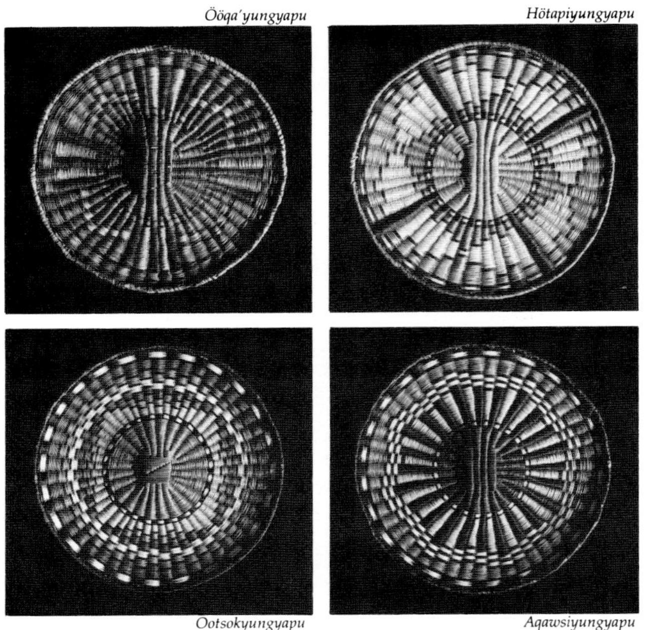

Ootsokyungyapu *Aqawsiyungyapu*

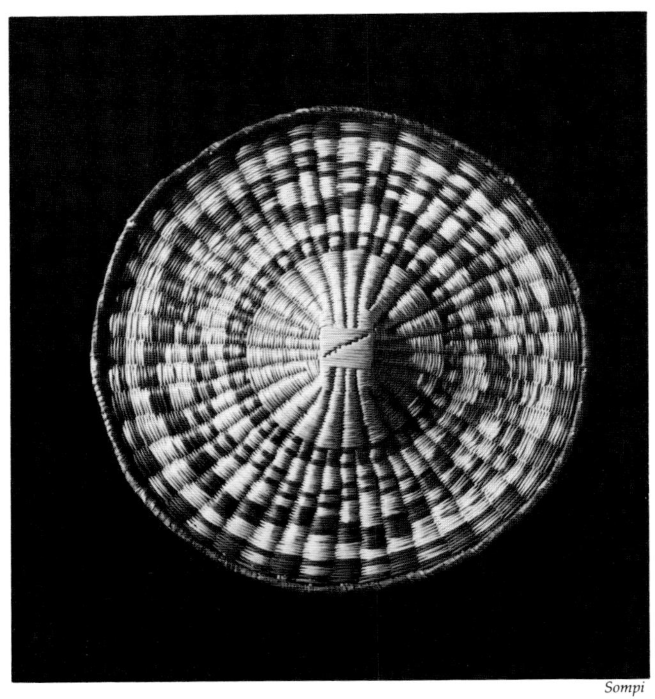

Sompi

Ööqa'yungyapu (bones wicker plaque) is an old plaque with a set of white parallel lines said to represent bones. No further interpretation was available.

Hötaapi means "device for opening" or "key" in Hopi, and this plaque is called a *hötapiyungyapu.* This is an obscure design; it is also puzzling: keys are not native to Hopi culture. Some observers believe that the stepped design element represents the large wooden keys of the Spanish.

Ootsokyungyapu means "filled-in" or "covered wicker plaque." This name refers to any plaque with a complex design that "fills-in" the surface of the plaque (except for a roughly rectangular portion in the center).

Sompi is "device for tying" in Hopi. This term is applied to plaques with two cords or "rope" designs running around the middle of the plaque.

Povolyungyapu *Tsilitosmoktaqa*

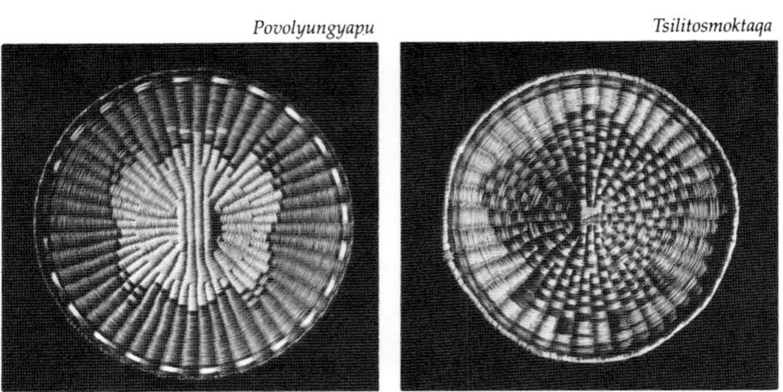

Poniyungyapu or *ponnikpu* (whirl wicker plaque) is commonly called a "whirlwind" plaque although this designation is a misnomer. Whirlwinds (tuviphayang) do not have positive connotations in Hopi and are not represented on plaques. The designs are simply whirls, and no interpretation of this design has been collected to date. A second term identified for this design is *yamomo* or "busy," referring to the complexity of the design. We do not know if the term applies to this design only or to any "busy" plaque. (See cover.)

Plant and Animal Motifs

Many plaques are named for the animals or plants represented by their dominant design element. Kwaayungyapu, for example, is the name for the plaque with the eagle (kwaahu) design. The plaque representing the butterfly is called *povolyungyapu*, and *aqawsiyungyapu* represents the sunflower.

Kachina Motifs

Today, many wicker plaques have representations of kachinas on them. These kachina plaques (katsinyungyapu) appear to be more common and varied today than at the turn of the century. One of the most common older forms of the katsinyungyapu is the representation of the *Tsilitosmoktaqa*, a runner-type kachina that carries a bag of hot chilis around his neck and challenges men to race with him. If he wins, the loser must eat the raw chili.

Angwusnasomtaqa (crow mother kachina) is another common kachina motif on plaques. This kachina appears at dawn on the final morning of the sixteen-day Bean Dance and carries a tray of bean sprouts. The Bean Dance is one of the major ceremonies of the Hopi calendar year. The germination and growth of beans in the kiva during the ceremony foretell the success of the coming year's crop.

ROBERT G. BREUNIG is Curator of Anthropology for the Museum of Northern Arizona.

The author would like to thank Michael Lomatu'wayma for help in preparing this article.

Reference

Voth, H. R.
1903 *The Oraibi Oa'göl Ceremony.* Field Columbian Museum, Publication 84, v. 6, n. 1.

Photograph: Emry Kopta Collection, MNA

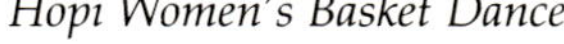
Hopi Women's Basket Dance

ONE HUNDRED YEARS OF HAVASUPAI BASKETRY

by Joyce Herold

The Havasupai have always been one of the most isolated of southwestern tribes, living and farming on the floor of a narrow, sheer-walled tributary of the Grand Canyon. Even in this day of helicopter accessibility, they still receive mail and most of their visitors over a precipitous eight-mile horse and foot trail. This remoteness has meant that only with difficulty, over a long period of time, have outsiders learned to appreciate this distinctive and tiny group of people, their lifeways, and their primary art form, basketry.

European knowledge of Havasupai culture began particularly slowly as the Southwest was explored by its Spanish and Anglo-American "discoverers." Though the Hopi and Zuni had traded for centuries with these canyon Indians, the first contact by a white man occurred in 1776 when Spanish missionary Francisco Tomás Garcés twice visited their Havasu (or Cataract) Canyon homeland. They were then left in isolation for almost two hundred years until their presence was noted by various American military, geological, and railroad exploring parties traversing northern Arizona in the mid-1880s. Still, the canyon remained a peaceful refuge, harboring not only the Havasupai but their Walapai relatives as well, during the latter's 1866–69 war with the whites. Only in the 1870s did prospectors begin to plague the Havasupai. To protect the 214 persons (60 men, 53 women, and 101 children) then living in the canyon and to preserve their lands, the government set up the Havasupai Reservation in 1880.

When Dr. Frank Hamilton Cushing, Curator of the Ethnological Department of the United States Museum, arrived the following year, he became the first white observer to seriously chronicle Havasupai life. Cushing quickly recognized his unique opportunity to record in depth this little known tribe—the "least acquainted with civilizations, perhaps, of any Indians in the United States." His efforts were greatly enhanced by the assistance of a Zuni interpreter-guide, whom the Havasupai considered a brother.

Cushing's account of his visit, published in two installments in the 1882 *Atlantic Monthly,* was the first detailed description of the canyon Indians to reach the public. One hundred years later, it stands as a landmark ethnographic record of an aboriginal culture on the verge of passing. The articles contain invaluable documentation on early Havasupai material culture—including one of its most important and interesting aspects, basketry.

During the centennial year of our outsiders' notice of this small but significant craft art complex, it seems appropriate to review our accumulated knowledge of Havasupai basketry, to honor its beginning and to note the major contributions that followed.

Basic Forms of Havasupai Basketry

Havasupai basketry has its roots in prehistoric Great Basin cultures and closely resembles early Paiute and Walapai examples. *Twined basketry* was the most common form of Supai utility container. These containers were made in a wide variety of styles including conical burden carriers held on the back by a tumpline; small-necked water bottles in round, squat, or bi-conical shapes; low, wide-mouthed globular bowls; and shallow circular trays. Each form of basketry was made in a wide range of sizes for use by small girls as well as women in their tasks of food gathering, storing, processing, and cooking.

Plain, diagonal, and three-ply twining techniques used twigs and split elements of catclaw (or alternately—squawberry, Fremont cottonwood, or willow). A coiled-on double round of twigs formed the rim. Melted piñon pitch was used to waterproof the jars, and fruit pulp or mescal leaf tissues were rubbed inside parching trays to make them heat resistant and to aid in waterproofing.

Decorative touches traditionally were simple and sparse. The alternated textures of the different twining stitches served as the primary ornamentation. These stitches were designed to strengthen as well as to ornament, which explains their presence even when pitch or other opaque coatings obscured them. Thin dentate, ticked, or linear encircling bands made from the split black covering of devil's claw pods often decorated Havasupai trays, bowls, and burden baskets.

Twined baskets changed little into the 1920s. They remained the basic cheap, readily made domestic containers for staple vegetal foods and water. However, commercial foods and metal vessels gradually became common, obviating the advantages of basketry for utility use. By mid-twentieth century, only smaller, cruder versions of twined baskets were being made—and these primarily for non-Indian customers.

Coiled ware formed the other traditional Havasupai fiber art. Though some coiled water jars, stone boiling jars, and drinking cups were made earlier, only late in the nineteenth century did Supai weavers turn toward a significant amount of coiling. They began making an attractive close-coiled, black-patterned basket tray (probably based on Yavapai prototypes), which quickly became an important dance basket trade item to the Hopis. Later, the Fred Harvey Company's Hopi House and other Indian shops at the Grand Canyon sold Havasupai "fancy baskets," which were always in shorter supply and more expensive than the quickly made Hopi baskets. The coiling of non-utilitarian baskets for sale became a "new tradition" at Supai, and by the 1930s, at the latest, coiling had supplanted twining in importance.

Shallow, medium- to large-sized circular trays have been the most characteristic coiled form, but plaques and oval bowls and trays are also distinctively Supai. The Havasupai basketmakers have produced many other forms—deep bowls, pedestal bowls, jars, and a variety of miniatures in limited numbers.

To make coiled ware, weavers sew squawberry, Fremont cottonwood, or willow elements (from a three-way twig split) counter-clockwise around a three-rod, triangular foundation of the same plant materials. Devil's claw strips form coiled-in designs. Average textures for these baskets, trays, and bowls are fifteen to nineteen stitches per inch, but extraordinarily fine textures of twenty-two to twenty-four stitches per inch were achieved during the 1930s, when technological expertise reached a peak.

A great complexity of geometric and representational designs (inspired by both traditional and imported sources) developed through time. More plant, animal, and other natural and cultural phenomena came to be used on baskets from the 1930s onward. Design layouts are most often encircling but can also be radiating, oblique, or repeated. Self- or false-braid rims are frequently plain, sometimes black, and occasionally ticked.

Havasupai coiling so closely resembles Walapai, Yavapai, Paiute, and Western Apache types that many Supai baskets probably have been classified with the more common Yavapai and Western Apache groups. It is readily distinguished only when several characteristic traits of form, rim, and design occur together in a basket.

Early Observations

Frank Hamilton Cushing's account of the Havasupai and their culture was rich and sensitive, yet ethnographically objective. In a period when writers heaped romantic praise and ethnocentric criticism alike on American Indians, Cushing tempered his judgments. The extremes reached in his treatment of Havasupai basketry are demonstrated in the following quotes. Supai women are "wonderfully apt and graceful in the use of the hand in making baskets," yet their art is "crude."

He observed that immense quantities of watertight basketry were produced in the 1880s, and he gave brief descriptions of utility baskets—descriptions that fit traditional twined types:

> . . . large, round, closely woven trays of basket work, coated with mineral asphaltum and earth, make excellent roasting pans.
>
> Large panniers, slung over the forehead or shoulders with a broad strap of raw-hide, are used in collecting food, or carrying it to and from the distant granaries; certain huge, small-necked, round-bottomed basket bottles serve as canteens and water-jars.
>
> Moqui bowls and native baskets are used in serving food.

Cushing also recognized at least some of basketry's significance as an art form:

> Possessing nothing but a rude architecture, their art is correspondingly crude, being mostly confined to the patterns on their basket-work and the paintings on their bows and arrows. The basket-work, by virtue of the regular arrangement of the splints, is often beautiful. But few people live, however, whose appreciation of art seems so great, compared with their limited practice of it.

This last unexplained sentence is perhaps the most tantalizing of Cushing's statements, for it is the earliest notation of how the Havasupais themselves feel about aesthetic matters. Unfor-

Representative trays, plaques, ollas, and bowls from the McKee Collection

Havasupai baskets collected by J. H. Bratley, 1900–01
Courtesy Denver Museum of Natural History

tunately, many years passed before another observer of Cushing's note paid any attention to Supai ethnoaesthetics.

In retrospect, we know that these early basket descriptions, discerning as they are, have several important failings. First, Cushing erred in his belief that the parching trays were "coated with mineral asphaltum and earth." In fact, the baskets were rubbed inside with crushed mescal leaf tissue, which appears claylike in stored ball form, or with peach pulp. Unfortunately, Cushing turned this small mistake into a significant one in his 1882–83 annual report when he not only elaborated the description with detailed drawings, but also based a theory of the origins of pottery on the supposed clay lining of baskets. Cushing's theory was widely quoted despite its apparent lack of verification through a collected specimen (none were found in Smithsonian collections of the day). Leslie Spier's definitive *Havasupai Ethnography* finally set the record straight in 1928.

Even more disappointing to art historians is Cushing's failure to delineate the techniques of basket weaving that he encountered. His nearest approach to descriptions of construction—"the regular arrangement of the splints"—seems to refer to twined ware, which he undoubtedly did observe. However, not one shred of evidence on coiled basketry occurs in the original report.

That this was a surprising oversight is made clear by his subsequent 1882–83 illustration and description of the Havasupai boiling basket—a bottle-shaped, spirally coiled vessel "still surviving as a sort of bucket." Coiling is also illustrated in his Havasupai roasting tray. Cushing accurately detailed the coiling process, however, and puzzlingly, he showed clockwise rather than the counter-clockwise coiling direction later thought to be invariable.

Both reports are vexingly silent about a crucial development postulated for the 1870–90 period. A new style of black-decorated coiled basketry was reportedly introduced by a Havasupai girl on her return from Yavapai captivity between 1870 and 1890. Although Cushing apparently saw none of these in 1881, we know the Supais had begun to produce (with the help of metal awls and larger domesticated devil's claw) their distinctive large ornamental trays by 1890 because they appear prominently in early Hopi photographs and collections.

Twentieth Century Observers

Shortly after Cushing's visit, the Grand Canyon became accessible by railroad and commercial tourist trips. From 1890 on, tourists were led by William Bass on the still-difficult ride to Cataract Canyon, and in 1892 a government farm and school were established at Supai village.

So began the trickle of observers of Havasupai basketry who followed Cushing. They included hundreds who adventured to the land of blue-green waters and saw, appreciated, purchased, and returned home with local souvenirs. Many gave these usually undocumented specimens to museums or mentioned the baskets in their travel accounts. But the best of the writings, photographs, and collections form a record from about 1900 to the present of the survival (with change) of a small, distinctive body of craft art, as well as of the Havasupai culture itself.

Important contributions to the story of Havasupai basketry come from Otis T. Mason, who included Havasupai notes based on the field observations of a variety of individuals and on analysis of Smithsonian collections in his 1902 compendium of Indian baskets. George Wharton James, a travel writer and basket fancier and hobbyist, highlighted Havasupai basketry in his 1903 book of personal observations, photographs, and interpretations, a book heavily larded with more substantive quotes from Mason. Leslie Spier, following his 1918, 1919, and 1921 fieldwork, wrote the classic Havasupai ethnography in which traditional twined utility ware was better described than ever before—but the newer commercial coiled ware was given short shrift.

Edwin McKee, Park Naturalist at the Grand Canyon during the 1930s, and Barbara McKee assembled a remarkably systematic collection of thirties' coiled baskets, which Joyce Herold later analyzed along with interviews with the surviving basketmakers, to produce a 1974 study emphasizing individual styles during the peak of coiling. Alfred F. Whiting wrote far-ranging 1942 Havasupai ethnobotanical notes, which remain unpublished. Also important to a complete understanding of Havasupai basketry were Bert Robinson, a southwestern Indian basketry collector; Carma Lee Smithson, a Utah ethnographer who in 1959 documented Havasupai women and their virtual loss of the old basket weaving ways in the changed post-war economy and society; and Paul Bateman, who focused on Walapai basketry change—with reference to the Havasupai—in an unpublished 1972 thesis.

In 1973 and 1974, I completed fieldwork that brought contemporary weavers and revival trends into the story. Finally, from all the above works and a study of additional collections, I attempted in 1974 and 1979 to clarify Havasupai basketry characteristics and to begin a synthesis of its history.

During this one-hundred-year period, appreciation of Supai basketry and basketmaking has grown, declined, and grown again to a present high public interest in the basketry and art of southwestern tribes. In these years, much has been discovered about the past and the unfolding themes and variation of the art.

Still, many rich areas remain little known or appreciated, awaiting new evidence and approaches. Perhaps, as they see their past afresh, new directions await the weavers themselves. May they join with other avid collectors and questing scholars to bring about an even more rewarding *bicentennial* of Havasupai basketry!

Joyce Herold, Curator of the department of anthropology for the Denver Museum of Natural History, has written extensively on the basketry of the Southwest.

BIBLIOGRAPHY

Bateman, Paul
1972 *Culture Change and Revival in Pai Basketry. Northern Arizona University, M.A. thesis.*

Cushing, Frank H.
1882 "The Nation of the Willows," *The Atlantic Monthly,* v. 5: 362–74, 541–59. Reprinted 1965, Northland Press, Flagstaff, Ariz.

Cushing, Frank H.
1886 "A Study of Pueblo Pottery as Illustrative of Zuni Culture Growth," *Smithsonian Institution, Bureau of*

American Ethnology, Annual Report (1882–83): 467–521.

Herold, Joyce
1979 "Havasupai Basketry, Theme and Variation," *American Indian Art Magazine,* v. 4, n. 4: 42–53.

James, George W.
1903 *Indian Basketry and How to Make Indian and Other Baskets.* Printed by the author, Pasadena, Calif.

Mason, Otis T.
1904 "Aboriginal American Basketry: Studies in a Textile Art without Machinery," *Smithsonian Institution, Bureau of American Ethnology, Annual Report* (1902): 171–548.

McKee, Barbara, Edwin D. McKee and Joyce Herold.
1975 *Havasupai Baskets and Their Makers: 1930–1940.* Northland Press, Flagstaff, Ariz.

Robinson, Bert
1954 *The Basket Weavers of Arizona.* University of New Mexico Press, Albuquerque, N. Mex.

Smithson, Carma L.
1959 "The Havasupai Woman," *Utah University Anthropological Papers* No. 38. University of Utah Press, Salt Lake City.

Spier, Leslie
1928 "Havasupai Ethnography," *American Museum of Natural History, Anthropological Papers 29:* (3). New York City.

Whiting, Alfred F.
1942 "Havasupai Habitat" Unpublished research manuscript. On file, Museum of Northern Arizona.

Photographic Credits

Deer, horse, and human designs in Havasupai coiled baskets. Page 14.

Havasupai twined parching and food trays. Page 15.

Baskets from the peak period of Havasupai coiling, showing superfine texture of 19 to 23 stitches per inch. Page 16.

Havasupai coiled baskets, 1930 to 1940. Page 17.

Havasupai baskets (circa 1900). Typical coiled trays, unusual lidded jar (showing rare use of aniline dye); twined food tray and seed jar. Page 18.

Design motifs from nature in coiled baskets spanning the century. Page 19.

Twined utility ware showing little change through time. Page 20.

All photographs courtesy of the Denver Museum of Natural History with special thanks to Edwin McKee

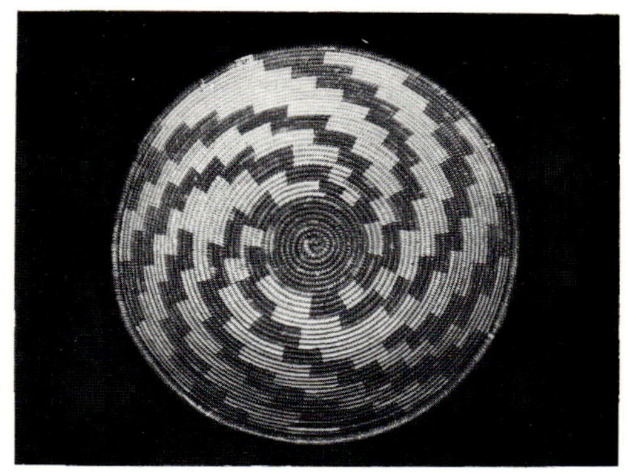

WESTERN APACHE BASKETS

by Clara Lee Tanner

Before 1850 numerous Apache Indian bands wandered over or close to the Colorado Plateau. Eventually, most of them (as well as other groups of Apaches) were settled on the Fort Apache (White Mountain) Reservation or on the San Carlos Reservation. During these years, Apaches came in frequent contact with other southwestern Indian tribes. About 1880, a number of Yavapais were placed on the San Carlos Reservation; some remained there until the turn of the century. This close contact between Apache and Yavapai may explain the many similarities, often to the point of confusion, between Apache and Yavapai baskets.

Apache legends refer to the ruins of cliff dwellings on the plateau, but these Indians did not know the ancient folk. They were, however, in direct contact with their lineal descendants, the puebloan people. It is possible that Apaches derived their basketry techniques and some vessel forms from the more sedentary groups they encountered. The Athapascan-speaking Apaches were notably adept at contact situations and cultural borrowing. Certainly they borrowed legends and many ritual ideas from the puebloans.

In the earliest years, Apache Indian women wove baskets for their own use or for trade with other Indians. Contacts between Indians and whites became fairly common with the coming of the railroads into the Southwest in the 1880s. Like other tribes of the area, the Apaches were encouraged to produce basketry for sale to these newcomers. This trade fostered a definite elaboration of pattern, a trend that was most outstanding from just before the turn of the century into the 1940s. Although substitutes for baskets in Apache homes began to appear before 1900, they became more and more abundant from the 1940s on, wiping out the use of most native pieces—except for the carrying basket. Today a few coiled baskets are woven, and the burden basket is produced in fair abundance for white trade, particularly in the San Carlos area.

The Western Apache have relied on two basic techniques (see pp. 5–7) for the production of their baskets, coiling and twining. In the first technique, willow or cottonwood, or in earlier years, mulberry, forms the foundation about which the same material is sewed or "coiled." Devil's claw or Martynia, a crawling desert plant, provides material for the black designs. The same materials, with the exception of devil's claw, and with the addition of squawberry, may be used for twined water jars and burden baskets. Whole rods are used for foundations in the splayed-out bottoms and carried onto side walls in an upright or vertical position, while the same material is split and used for the filler or weaving element. Most commonly, two of the latter are woven simultaneously, one over, one under the foundation and twined between them. Both coiled and twined weaves are well executed (tight and close together) in the baskets of both groups.

Both White Mountain and San Carlos Apaches have added the use of non-vegetal materials to color their baskets. Red, black, blue, or blue-green designs on burden baskets may involve several different dye sources—some of native vegetal origin, some aniline dyes. The black coloring found on water jars usually is derived from soot. Both groups have used buckskin on burden baskets for bottom patches, for four vertical bands on wide walls, and for thongs on (and often between) bands. Chamois was substituted for buckskin in later years. Hair (usually horsehair), leather, and wood are the primary materials used to make water jars or burdens. Carrying straps are then attached to these loops. The straps themselves are usually made of leather or horsehair. Apache basketmakers often rubbed ground leaves into the interstices of water jars to aid in waterproofing. A final material, pitch from the piñon tree, was then melted and spread over the inside and outside of the water jar for more complete waterproofing.

The star or flowerlike theme is one of the most-favored Western Apache designs.

Styles of Western Apache Basketry

Western Apache baskets may be divided into a few fundamental styles. In general, deviations from basic forms are more common among the San Carlos weavers than among those of the White Mountain area; many of these deviations are slight but observable. Perhaps some variations began as a response to needs; many more reflect the artistry or even the whims of the weaver. Traditionally, jars, the burden "bucket" baskets, and trays were the dominant forms of both groups although a few bowls also were woven.

The coiled tray was an all-purpose basket—used for mixing and serving foods, washing, holding objects and materials, and, no doubt, for numerous other purposes. Deepened and with straighter sides, the tray became a bowl, a form more useful for holding liquids. Generally, bowls show less variation in shape than do trays.

Western Apache basketmakers usually made both twined and coiled jars with constricted mouth-neck areas and full bodies. Although variations occurred in jars of both weaves, they were more frequent in the coiled piece—perhaps because it was made for sale. Water jars show some variety in construction. Many had simple rounded bodies; others had high and wide shoulders, while some were straight-sided with a wide, flat bottom. More rarely, an hourglass form was featured in this twined jar. Mouths on water jars tended to be simple. They were wider on the larger, stationary pieces used for water storage, narrow on the smaller ones in which water was carried. Generally, the mouth wall sloped slightly outward from base to rim, and the neck was of medium height. Occasionally, the shape varied.

Coiled jars, on the other hand, presented many variations. Height, for example, ranged from about one foot to five feet. Bodies were gently rounded from neck to base, with high, sharp shoulders, or with not-so-high rounded ones. Some were slightly, some greatly, constricted toward midwall. Coiled jars exhibited graceful lines from top to a small base or more awkward ones from wide top to wide base. Adding to all this variety was the neck, which varied from tall to short and wide to narrow or was straight from base to rim or woven with a slight or great outcurve. There also were differences in the juncture of neck and body; these included gently or abruptly curved, depressed, flowing, as well as others. Innumerable combinations of all of these features resulted in a wide variety of shapes for these jars.

Lifeforms—men and animals—are coupled with various geometric elements —zigzags and triangles.

The popular central star motif banded by zigzags and crosses

The trays of the Western Apache were often small in earlier years although quite a few larger ones were woven later. Almost all these trays have sloping sides—some gently so, some more abrupt. Straight sides are uncommon early and late, while a gentle curve from rim to a wider or narrower base prevails.

Since the burden basket was used to haul a variety of objects (from foodstuffs to wood), its form featured a serviceable wide mouth and a wide base. There is little variation in this form although some burdens were shorter in relation to width than others. In the 1970s, base measurement became smaller in proportion to the rim, creating an almost-cone. This shape was made almost exclusively for sale.

It is quite likely that many early Apache baskets were undecorated, for those woven in the 1880s reveal sparse pattern that is scattered out over the surface of trays. Most known early baskets of other southwestern tribes also are undecorated or have limited designs.

Designs and Patterns

Design in Western Apache basketry is related to technology, form, and use. In twined water

A twined water bottle with banded neck and body

Radiating diamonds unify the center of this basket with the rim.

bottles, there is little or no pattern except for some lines or bands in three elements woven against the basic two-element weave. These bands may have been first a strengthening expedient and second a decorative device, for the patterning often appears at points of stress, such as the turn from base onto wall. Otherwise, there are rare black designs of a simple nature, such as a single black band made with a finger dipped in crushed charcoal. This pattern generally is applied before the pitching process—making it more or less permanent.

Although the banded design predominates on burden baskets, it appears in great variety. Two to as many as seven bands may appear on the wide walls of a basket of this form. Bands may be of the same size or varied in width; they may be bound at each edge with a line of solid color or a broken line—or the band may be open on one or both edges. The same motif or motifs may appear in all bands, or the same design is in top and bottom rows with different ones in between.

Patterns in the decorative bands of burden baskets are basically simple and small geometrics—with lines, squares, triangles, and solid bands most common as well as a scattering of diamonds. Lines may be long and encircling, single or multiple, or short verticals or diagonals. Squares may be repeated within the band or in several rows that suggest checkers, appear at the edge or edges as cogwheels, or even occur in diagonal step arrangements. Triangles also show great variety. They point up or down in repetitive or alternating rows, are large and widely spaced pendants, or touch tips to form hourglass themes.

Color adds a further dimension to these basically simple patterns. Often, all designs on a single basket are expressed in red, red-brown, or black, alone or in combination. Black and red short diagonal lines interchange in a band, or stitches in a line do the same. A solid red band may recur between black-designed bands; touching black and red diagonals are separated by natural diagonals. Other possibilities include squat black triangles interrupting an otherwise solid red band and stitching that outlines a geometric, such as an open diamond. Rarely blue-green appears.

No lifeforms were noted on Western Apache

twined burden baskets until 1980, when single deer designs were repeated four times in a band with geometrics above and below. In 1981 quite a few more such baskets were decorated with comparable lifeforms, suggesting the development of a new pattern.

Western Apache baskets in coiled weave feature a wide variety of designs. These are made up of the smallest parts of pattern called elements or units; motifs, which usually combine several elements; and the total pattern involving all elements and motifs used to weave a basket. Common elements run the gamut from lines to life figures and include dots, bands, lines, squares, rectangles, triangles, diamonds, solid circles, and occasional odd forms. Frequently, lifeforms appear alone as distinct entities. These are often treated as units of design despite the fact that they are built up of squares, rectangles, and lines. The most common lifeforms in Apache basketry are men, horses, dogs, and deer.

Motifs include single or multiple stars or flowers and stacked or spiraling rows of any of the geometric units—plus zigzags, checkerboarding, steps large or small, crosses, rows of animals or humans, and some large and odd or complex geometrics. Some baskets are decorated with a single motif, some with two or three—often with small elements, particularly lifeforms, thrown in here and there.

Very important to a discussion of Western Apache basketry is the variety in pattern arrangement (or layout). The most popular styles feature all-over, banded, half-banded, centered, or organizational banded detailing. All-over layouts have integrated pattern over the entire vessel surface. Banded layout may be all-over or spaced out; in both situations, design elements are enclosed by parallel lines. Half-banded styles have a single line from which the pattern is pendant while organizational banded has no bordering lines—but the design simulates a band, such as a continuous fret. Centered compositions may be simple or complex and grow out of the central black circle that is a dominant design element in a majority of Western Apache coiled baskets.

Photograph courtesy of Don and Nita Hoel

An unusual oval shape with standard Western Apache designs

Composite styles of layout would include a combination of any two or more of these; for example, one Apache tray can feature centered, banded, and organizational banded layouts.

An interesting adaptation of design to space occurs in the Western Apache coiled jar. In a majority of instances, design continues from body onto neck. Often, there is a smaller repetition of the body theme on the neck. On basket jars with a high and pronounced shoulder, the motif on the upper part of the shoulder sometimes differs from that of the body. This shoulder motif is then repeated on the neck.

There are both vertical and horizontal arrangements of pattern on the bodies of these jars. Most commonly, they feature all-over pattern—either with joined rectangles, solid triangles with multiple outlines, large vertically touching solid or outline diamonds, or repeated stepped diagonals. Sometimes, two vertical themes alternate. Although not as numerous, horizonal design schemes (such as separate or touching rows of zigzags, solid or lighter triangles, or rows of triangles alternating with checkers) do occur.

Small geometrics and lifeforms frequently are thrown in to supplement the more massive geometric patterns. They are added in repetitive fashion wherever there is room. Sometimes they appear within black triangles or diamonds—or they are enclosed by single or multiple outlines of large geometrics.

Despite these many orderly compositions, there are occasional helter-skelter arrangements of similar small elements. In addition to this lapse in order in the small patterns on coiled jars, there is an occasional "slip" in large designs. There may be an extra—and one only—zigzag or other theme dropped halfway down from the neck and between the more orderly arrangements of stacked diamonds.

One last detail of jar decoration is the design on the base. This involves both simple and complex themes—from a small center circle with a ring beyond it to an elaborate scheme such as an inner circle with eight projecting triangles. This wealth of detail suggests that these coiled jars were made for sale rather than native use, for wear on the base design from the wickiup's dirt floor would have been great. Few jars with elaborate base design indicate any hard use.

The shapes of coiled bowls sometimes affected the arrangement of design; for example, a straight-sided piece might have separate bottom and wall decoration. However, it is likely that tray styles affected bowl patterns since design was frequently unified from basket center to the rim.

Apache coiled tray designs are a delight, for they are extremely varied in layout and design. Some are quiet and static; some are so dynamic that design seems to continue beyond the basket edge. Practically all are in black on a natural background; red is rarely used. A sampling of these basketry patterns reveals much about Western Apache decoration.

Banded patterns tend toward the static, particularly where there is a plain black center with two or three spaced-out bands of checkers between it and the rim. But even this theme is occasionally enlivened by the addition of zigzags between bands. Some bands are organizational with regular bands between them. Such combinations create composite layouts, but if they touch, the result is an all-over plan.

Quite static also are stacked geometrics moving straight out from a center circle to the rim. Four, six, or more rows of solid plain or outlined triangles or diamonds may be so arranged. Between such rows, Western Apache basketmakers occasionally place a second and lesser motif—such as smaller diamonds or scattered units such as lifeforms or crosses—none of these offering motion to the heavily static design.

Spiraling steps or zigzags are very dynamic. They are designed with short and/or long steps of double or triple lines and may have deep or shallow zigzags. These designs may or may not touch the center circle but almost always touch the rim. Four, five, or even six of these moving "arms" create dramatic all-over patterning—sometimes very crowded, sometimes more spaced out.

One of the most favored Western Apache designs is the star or flowerlike theme. Those with four or five points or petals are most common, but some designs have six or more. Basketmakers created a single centered solid or outline style on some trays. On others, they chose two separate double outline flowers or two or three of the same outlines with each one extending from the tips of the previous petals. Sometimes a secondary motif, such as a partial row of stacked small triangles, appears toward the center, or lifeforms are placed between rows of petals.

Other arrangements of design occur but less frequently. Half-bands, such as triangles pen-

dant from a line, usually appear with another style—banded, for example; the result is a composite layout. Centered schemes, such as a center circle with various units attached, are not uncommon. They most typically show five triangles joined to the circle to form a star. Other geometrics and lifeforms may be treated in a similar manner.

Apache Basketry

Whether static or dynamic, Apache patterns are always interesting. The Apache weaver invariably creates a motif peculiarly her own even though she uses the same units as another tribeswoman. Sometimes the units themselves are distinctly Apache. For example, the tops of triangles might be flat, but the two sides can be gently and gracefully curved. The same is true of the "Apache diamonds," which are often pleasingly outcurved on the upper portions and incurved on the lower sides.

Another typically Apache trait is the apparently casual and random "throwing in" of lifeforms or small geometrics between large geometric motifs. Often these are irregular in number, form, or position. In one basket, for example, a man and dog stand between stacked triangles in eight spots—but the dog is missing in the ninth section, and all the dogs except one face the men. In many tray designs, all male figures except one will have their arms down at their sides; the exception has one arm upraised. This deviation may suggest the basketmaker's boredom, or it may be an attempt to express originality.

The trays of the Western Apache reflect the general history of their basketry. Forms were simple and limited until just before the turn of the century. Trays then began to show substantial diversity until about 1940, when they became simpler again. In the years between 1940 and 1981, trays were simple in form and limited in production. Overall design follows the same general scheme, with the peak of creativity, variety, and richness of expression occurring between 1890 and 1940. Today, the burden basket, with its changing form and the introduction of life designs on its walls for the first time, is the best example of a craft art that retains its potential for originality and freshness.

CLARA LEE TANNER, Professor Emeritus in the department of anthropology at the University of Arizona, has spent over forty years studying southwestern Native American crafts.

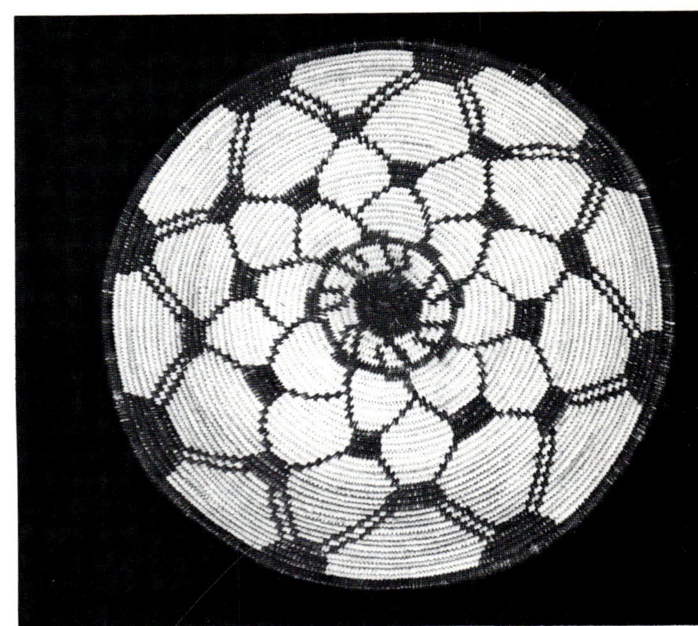

An all-over net design radiates from the ce

NOTE: This material is taken in part from a book on Apache basketry to be published in 1982 by the University of Arizona Press.

Photographic Credits

On burden baskets, banded geometric designs and buckskin fringe with metal tinklers are quite common. Page 22.
An all-over net design with men and animals situated around the body of the jar. Page 31.

All photographs not otherwise credited from the collections of the Museum of Northern Arizona.

COUNTY of Coconino STATE of Arizona

Statement of Ownership, Management and Circulation of PLATEAU as required by the Act of Congress of August 12, 1970, Section 3685, Title 39, United States Code:

1. That the frequency of publication is quarterly.
2. That the location of known office of publication is Museum of Northern Arizona, Rt. 4, Box 720, Flagstaff, Arizona.
3. That the location of the headquarters or general business offices of the publishers is Museum of Northern Arizona, Rt. 4, Box 720, Flagstaff, Arizona.
4. That the name and address of the Owner and Publisher is Museum of Northern Arizona, Rt. 4, Box 720, Flagstaff, Arizona 86001.
5. That the Editor is Diana Lubick, c/o Rt. 4, Box 720, Flagstaff, Arizona 86001.
6. That there are no stockholders, bondholders, mortgagees or other security holders.

ss. Robert A. Bow
Director

Designed by Pamela Scott Lungé. Typography by Stanley Stillion.

FRONT COVER: *Poniyungyapu (Whirl Wicker Plaque) from the collections of the Museum of Northern Arizona. Maker: Eva Dahwyeoma, Hotevilla, 1949.*